COUNTRY · EXPLORERS ·

A Visit to

FINLAND

by Charis Mather

BEARPORT
PUBLISHING

Minneapolis, Minnesota

Credits

All images are courtesy of Shutterstock.com, unless otherwise specified. With thanks to Getty Images, Thinkstock Photo, and iStockphoto.

Cover – Roman Babakin, S-F. 2 – BlueOrange Studio. 4–5 – Bee-man, ixpert. 6–7 – petch one, LBSimms Photography, mapsandphotos, Oleksiy Mark. 8–9 – Artem Babenov, Dainis Derics. 10–11 – Ruslan Kalnitsky, Popova Tetiana. 12–13 – Tsuguliev, Frozenmost. 14–15 – Paulharding00, footageclips. 16–17 – PhotoJanski, elina. 18–19 – Mr. Tempter, Kzenon. 20–21 – kallevalkama, Adam Major, Rawpixel.com. 21 – NordicImages, Alamy Stock Photo. 22–23 – Katrinshine, Suratwadee Rattanajarupak.

Library of Congress Cataloging-in-Publication Data is available at www.loc.gov or upon request from the publisher.

ISBN: 979-8-88509-372-9 (hardcover)
ISBN: 979-8-88509-494-8 (paperback)
ISBN: 979-8-88509-609-6 (ebook)

© 2023 Booklife Publishing
This edition is published by arrangement with Booklife Publishing.

For more information, write to Bearport Publishing, 5357 Penn Avenue South, Minneapolis, MN 55419.

CONTENTS

COUNTRY TO COUNTRY

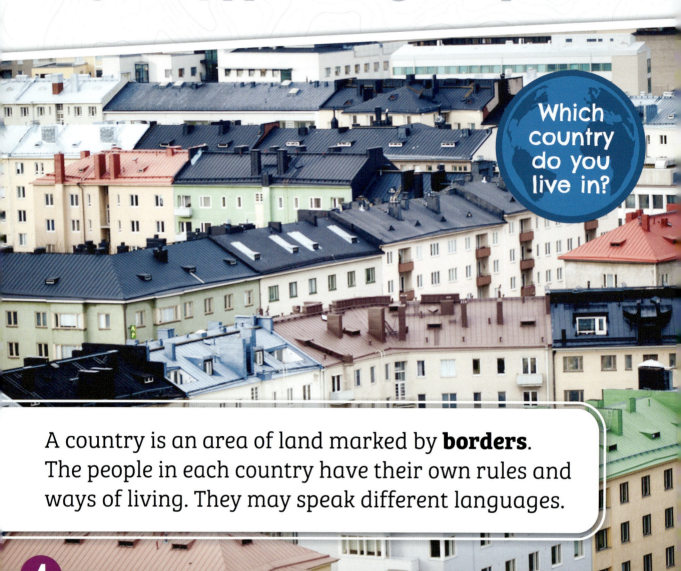

Which country do you live in?

A country is an area of land marked by **borders**. The people in each country have their own rules and ways of living. They may speak different languages.

Each country around the world has its own interesting things to see and do. Let's take a trip to visit a country and learn more!

Have you ever visited another country?

TODAY'S TRIP IS TO
FINLAND!

Finland is a country in the **continent** of Europe.

FACT FILE

Capital city: Helsinki
Main languages:
Finnish and Swedish
Currency: Euro
Flag:

Currency is the type of money that is used in a country.

HELSINKI

We'll start our trip in Finland's capital city, Helsinki. We can visit many beautiful buildings there, including the Uspenski Cathedral.

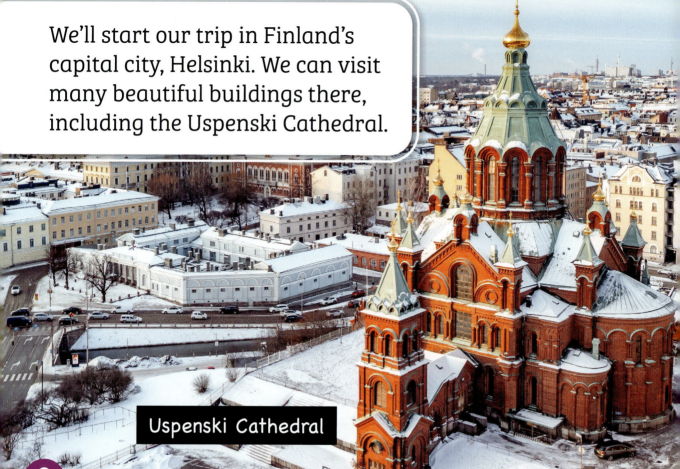

Uspenski Cathedral

We can also take a boat to visit forests and beaches on Helsinki's **archipelago** (ahr-kuh-PEL-uh-goh). This string of 300 islands is just a small amount of the 70,000 islands that are part of Finland.

9

SUOMENLINNA FORTRESS

These walls were made to fit on rocky land.

Some of Helsinki's islands have stone walls that zigzag on the edges of the land. The walls are part of Suomenlinna **Fortress**, which protected Helsinki long ago.

Now, hundreds of people live around the fortress. There are also many people who travel to see it. They can learn about Suomenlinna's past while enjoying its parks and tunnels.

NORTHERN LIGHTS

Finland is one of the most northern countries in the world. In places this far north, people can sometimes see **natural** glowing colors in the sky when it is dark. These are known as the northern lights.

The northern lights are also called the aurora borealis.

In parts of Finland, the northern lights can be seen about 200 nights a year. The lights are often bright green, purple, or yellow.

SÁMI PEOPLE

The most northern part of Finland is home to many Sámi people. They were the first group of people to ever live in this country.

The Sámi people are known for **herding** reindeer. Sometimes, they ride sleds or **skis** pulled by the animals.

MIDSUMMER

Time to celebrate! One of Finland's most important holidays is Midsummer. It celebrates the day of the year with the most sunlight.

Finnish people often celebrate Midsummer by making fires outside.

On this day, the sun is even out at night! It's called the Midnight Sun. To celebrate Midsummer, people swim under this nighttime sun.

Some Finnish people dance to celebrate Midsummer.

SAUNAS

Being in a sauna can help people relax.

Next, let's go sit in a sauna! These wooden, **steam**-filled rooms are very popular in Finland. Because saunas are hot, people stay in them for only a short time.

There are millions of saunas in Finland. Some are open to anyone. People may go to these shared saunas with friends or family. Other saunas are in people's homes.

Some Finnish people go to shared saunas every week.

PYHÄ-LUOSTO NATIONAL PARK

Look at that view! Pyhä-Luosto National Park has beautiful forests. There are also high-up areas with no trees. These areas are called fells.

Many people ski over the snow-covered fells. Others use snowshoes to walk! These wide, flat shoes stop people from sinking into snow.

A snowshoe

BEFORE YOU GO

We can't forget to try some Finnish food! Let's grab some Karelian pies. These **pastries** are filled with rice porridge. They are often eaten for breakfast or as a snack.

Karelian pie

We could also visit Porvoo. This is one of the oldest towns in Finland. Many people go there to see the bright-red wooden houses that sit on the edge of a river.

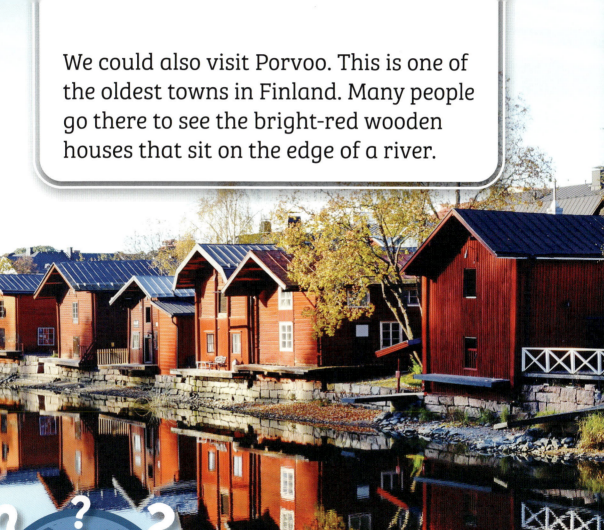

What have you learned about Finland on this trip?

GLOSSARY

archipelago a group of islands

borders lines that show where one place ends and another begins

continent one of the world's seven large land masses

fortress a place built to handle attacks

herding gathering a large group of animals

natural not made by humans

pastries a baked food made of dough that often has a filling

skis long, flat attachments to shoes used for gliding quickly on top of snow

steam a mist that forms from hot water

INDEX